MAKE
PLASTIC
FANTASTIC

Over 25 recycling craft projects

AUTUMN PUBLISHING

AUTUMN
PUBLISHING

Written by fairandfunky
(Sophie Bebb and Helen Robinson)

Illustrated by DGPH
(Diego Vaisberg and Martin Lowenstein)

Designed by Richard Sykes
Edited by Helen Catt

An imprint of Igloo Books Group,
part of Bonnier Books UK
bonnierbooks.co.uk

Published in 2020
by Igloo Books Ltd, Cottage Farm
Sywell, NN6 0BJ

Manufactured in China. 0320 001
10 9 8 7 6 5 4 3 2 1

Library of Congress Cataloging-in-Publication
Data is available upon request.

ISBN 978-1-83852-391-6
autumnpublishing.co.uk
bonnierbooks.co.uk

About the author

Helen Robinson and Sophie Bebb established fairandfunky, a community interest company with the mission statement: empowering people to take their own little steps to change the world. They deliver interactive and creative workshops to schools and community groups, run events, host SCRAPtastic community workshops, and are the go-to organization for local and global sustainability education in Yorkshire, UK. They believe that all individuals have the power to make a positive difference in the world: through the way we act, what we wear, where we shop, and what we do.

WHOOOSH!

CONTENTS

CRAFTING TOP TIPS

Here are some quick and easy tips to help you make the most of the crafts in this book. Read these before you dive in!

1. Keep a lookout for supplies.

Check what you need for each craft before you start. If you're missing something, ask your friends and family. Chances are someone you know would be throwing it away, anyway. Picnics and birthday parties are good places to check—there are often lots of big plastic bottles and plastic cups you can ask to take home.

2. Use what you have.

If you come across something in the instructions that you really can't find, don't go out and buy it specially! This book is packed with ideas for how to reuse the things you would normally get rid of, so buying something new defeats the point. Look around for something else you can use instead. Use your imagination. If you can't find colored cellophane, would painted newspaper work just as well?

3. Use ALL of what you have.

Where a craft only uses half of a bottle, don't throw the other half away. Is there a craft you can do that uses the other half?

4

4. Clean your materials THOROUGHLY.

Ask a grown-up to help you wash out any plastic food or drinks containers in warm, soapy water before you use them. Everything should be clean and dry when you start crafting.

5. Prepare to get messy.

Lots of these crafts use paint or liquid glue. Make sure you're wearing old clothes or an apron. Do the crafts outside or cover the table and floor with old newspaper or plastic—cut along one side and the bottom of a big plastic trash bag and unfold it to make a quick waterproof tablecloth!

6. Keep your grown-up nearby.

Grown-ups are useful for using sharp scissors and helping with any tricky parts. Make sure they know what you're doing and that they read through the warning on this page before you start.

⚠ Note for grown-ups

Some of the crafts in this book involve potential hazards such as sharp implements or allergens. The publisher strongly recommends that parents and guardians supervise their children during ALL activities, paying particular attention to stages marked with a warning sign.

Whenever starting out on one of these crafts, always read through the instructions and consider what safety precautions are necessary before you start. Always use your judgement and stay safe.

TOYS AND GAMES

ZAAAP!

Why buy a new toy with lots of plastic packaging when you can make something better? Learn to juggle with cool, colorful juggling balls made of old plastic bags or make a set of alien puppets that are out of this world. From castles to kites, there's plenty to keep you busy!

FLOWER CATCH GAME

Have you heard the buzz? This flower catcher game is un-BEE-lievable. How many times can you use the flower to catch the bee without missing? Can you BEE-t your friends' records?

YOU WILL NEED

- 1.5 liter plastic bottle
- scissors
- marker
- colored card
- holepunch
- liquid glue
- tissue paper
- cork
- thin black ribbon
- sticky tape

STEP 1

Measure 4.5 inches from the bottom of the plastic bottle. Mark several points around the bottle, then join up the points to draw a line all around the bottle. Ask a grown-up to help you cut along the line.

STEP 2

Discard the bottom part of the bottle (use it to do one of the other crafts in this book). Draw five petal shapes around the edge of the top part of the bottle and carefully cut them out.

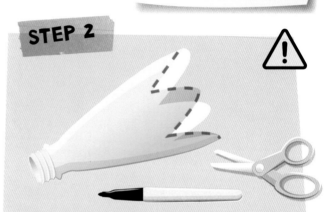

STEP 3

Fold the petals back on themselves so they stick out at right angles to the rest of the bottle.

STEP 4

Mix up a solution that is one part liquid glue, one part water. Tear up pieces of green and orange tissue paper. One by one, dip the pieces of tissue paper into the glue mix and stick them to the bottle, using orange for the petals and green for the rest of the flower.

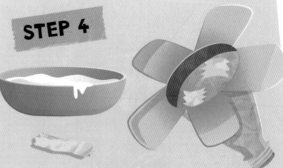

8

STEP 5

Fold a small piece of card in half and cut out a rounded shape for the wings. Use a holepunch to make a hole about half a centimeter from the fold line. Then cut out other shapes of card to make the bee's face.

STEP 6

Stick the card shapes onto the front of the cork, arranging them to make a face. Cut some short lengths of ribbon and stick them onto the bee's body to make its stripes. Then thread a piece of ribbon 20 inches long through the two holes in the wing shapes and tie it tightly around the bee's body.

BZZZ!

STEP 7

Thread the end of the ribbon through the bottom of the bottle and tie it around the bottle's neck. Add some sticky tape to secure it. Your catch game is ready to play!

JUGGLING JUMBLES

Quit clowning around and get to work making these juggling balls. They're ideal for first-time jugglers, as they move slowly through the air and don't bounce or roll if they're dropped. Use lots of different colored plastic bags to make a set of colorful juggling balls, then use the guide opposite to learn how to juggle.

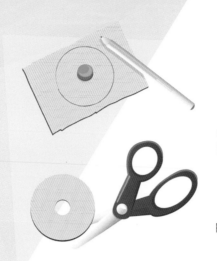

YOU WILL NEED

- plenty of plastic bags
- stiff card
- scissors
- string

Find two round objects, one a bit bigger than the other, such a mug and a plastic lid. Draw around them onto the card so that you have two circles, one inside the other. Cut them out so you have a ring shape made of card. Repeat this step so you have two identical rings.

STEP 2

Cut along a plastic bag, starting at the bottom and cutting around in circles all the way up the bag, to make a long, thin ribbon. Wind it into a ball as you go along so it doesn't get tangled.

STEP 3

Place the two rings back to back. Wrap the plastic ribbon around the rings, feeding it through the middle and around the outside. Keep wrapping it until the whole ring is covered in lots of layers of plastic.

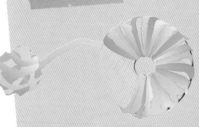

STEP 4

Carefully slip your scissors between the two cardboard rings and snip along the outer edge. Make sure you only cut the plastic around the outside, and not in the middle part.

HOW TO JUGGLE

1

Stand with your elbows bent at right angles. Make sure there's nothing breakable nearby! Start with one ball in one hand. Throw it just above eye level to your opposite hand. Try to catch it with a slight scooping motion and immediately throw it back to your starting hand, so the catch-scoop-throw makes one smooth action. Practice until you can throw to the same height every time with both hands.

STEP 5

Ease the cardboard rings slightly apart. Slip a piece of string (or another piece of plastic ribbon) between the two rings. Tie it tightly.

2

Now go on to using two balls. Start with one in each hand. Throw the first ball as you did before. Just when it reaches the top of the arc, throw the second ball. Its path should stay just inside the path of the first ball. Practice until you can do 10–12 throws with each hand without stopping or dropping.

STEP 6

Cut the cardboard rings, being careful not to cut either the string or the plastic. Take the cut rings off the juggling ball. Use scissors to carefully trim any uneven bits (as if you're giving it a haircut). Make two more to make a full set of juggling balls.

3

You're ready to juggle with three balls. Start with two in one hand and one in the other. Starting with the hand with two balls, throw the balls as you did before. This time, just as you catch the first ball, and when the second ball reaches the top of the arc, throw the third ball. When the third ball reaches the top of the arc, and just as you catch the second ball, throw the first ball again. Then just keep going!

MONSTER PINS

Make these monstrous pins. They're an absolute SCREAM. Use a tennis ball or make a mini-version of the quick football on page 54 to bowl them over.

page 54

YOU WILL NEED

- 6 small, identical plastic bottles
- tissue paper
- liquid glue
- colored card
- scissors
- 300g sand or uncooked rice

STEP 1

Mix up one part liquid glue to one part water. Tear up strips of tissue paper and dip them into the mix. Then paste them onto the plastic bottles. You can make each monster a different color, or make them all multicolored. Leave the tops of the bottles (where the lids screw on) clear.

STEP 2

Draw and cut out a selection of eyes, hands, tentacles, mouths, and teeth for your monsters. Use colored card, or use an old cereal box and paint it.

STEP 3

Arrange your monsters' faces. Make them as scary or silly as you like. Use liquid glue to paste all the pieces in place.

STEP 4

Pour 50g of sand or uncooked rice into each one of the bottles, and put the caps on tightly. This weighs down the bottom of the monsters to make them trickier to knock over. You can use more or less sand depending on how easy you want your bowling game to be.

HOW TO PLAY

Take turns with a friend to stand 15 paces away and throw a ball to knock over the pins. Keep score and see who's knocked over the most pins after 10 throws.

CRAAASH!

CRAFTY CASTLE

Once you've made this castle, you can try making even bigger castles. Gather as many different bottles as you can find and arrange them into the shape you want your castle to be. You can use spooky colors to make a witch's or wizard's castle or fairy-tale colors to make a fairy castle.

YOU WILL NEED

- plastic bottles
- liquid glue
- scissors
- gray or silver tissue paper
- paint
- toothpicks
- scrap card

STEP 1

Arrange your bottles to make a castle shape. Use two tall bottles for the castle towers, two smaller bottles for the gatehouse towers, and a flat-fronted bottle (like a mouthwash bottle) for the front of the castle.

STEP 2

Tear up strips of tissue paper. Dip them into a mix of one part glue, one part water and paste them onto the bottle, overlapping slightly.

STEP 3

While the bottles are drying, make your decorations. Draw shapes on cardboard, carefully cut them out, and paint them. You might want to make doors, windows, flags, trailing plants, and crenellations for the tops of the castle walls.

STEP 4

Glue the two castle towers together. Use liquid glue to attach the toothpicks to the flags, then stick the flags to the tops of the castle towers. Add some windows and some crenellations to the tops of the towers.

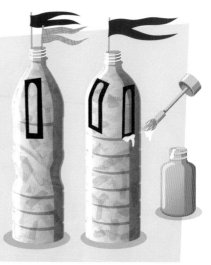

STEP 5

Glue one of the smaller bottles either side of the flat-fronted bottle. To the gatehouse towers, stick on the trailing vines and some brick shapes. Stick the door onto the front of the castle and add crenellations to the tops of all the bottles.

STEP 6

Cut out a rectangle of cardboard the width of the two castle towers. Cover with liquid glue and stick to the front of the castle towers. You may have to hold it in place while it dries.

STEP 7

Add glue to the other side of the cardboard and stick the three smaller bottles to it to complete your castle. Again, you may want to hold the bottles in place while the glue dries.

BALLOON ROCKET

YOU WILL NEED

- small plastic bottle
- liquid glue
- tin foil
- colored card
- red and yellow plastic film
- long balloon
- clothespin
- straw
- sticky tape
- string

For this rocket launch, you'll need a large, clear area with something at each end to attach your string to, like a tree or a doorknob. The lighter your plastic bottle is, the better this rocket will work. How far can you make your rocket "fly"?

WHOOOSH!

STEP 1

First, cover the plastic bottle with tin foil, using liquid glue to stick it down.

STEP 2

Decorate your rocket with fins and portholes made out of colored card. Cut flame shapes out of the red and yellow plastic film and stick them to the bottom of the rocket.

STEP 3

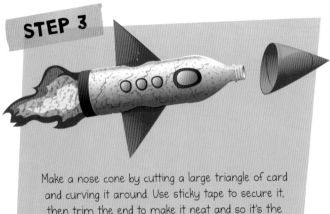

Make a nose cone by cutting a large triangle of card and curving it around. Use sticky tape to secure it, then trim the end to make it neat and so it's the right width to fit on the top of the bottle.

STEP 4

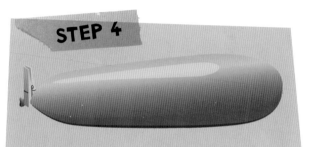

Take your long balloon and blow it up. Twist the end tightly and secure it with the clothespin so all the air stays in.

STEP 5

Place two pieces of sticky tape so they're facing upward and stick the straw on top. Place two more pieces of sticky tape on top of the straw, so they're facing downward (be careful not to stick them to the other tape or to the table).

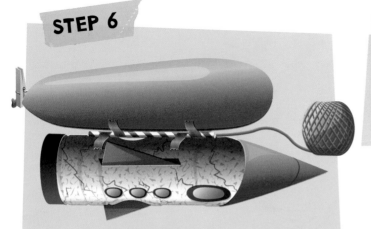

STEP 6

Use the downward facing sticky tape to attach the straw to the back of the rocket. Use the upward facing sticky tape to attach the straw to the balloon. Thread a long piece of string through the straw.

STEP 7

Tie the string to something at each end so the string is horizontal. Move the rocket to the end of the string, count down from 10, then release the clothespin to launch.

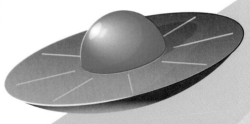

ALIEN PUPPETS

Use lots of funny-shaped bottles and bright colors to create a whole planet of different aliens. They can walk, run, dance, and even chase each other across alien landscapes. With a few props, a video camera, and a space background, you can even use them to make your own super sci-fi movie.

YOU WILL NEED

- 16 oz plastic bottle
- paint
- 4 bottle lids
- chunky yarn
- thread
- colored card
- scissors
- liquid glue
- 2 stiff straws

STEP 1

Decorate your bottle with colored paint. This will be your alien's body. Paint your bottle lids. These will be the alien's hands and feet. You can use whatever colors you like, depending how you want your alien to look.

STEP 2

Ask your grown-up to poke a small hole in each of the bottle lids. Thread a 6 inch length of yarn through the top of each bottle cap, then tie a knot in each end of the yarn.

STEP 3

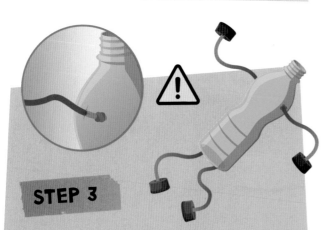

Cut four small, narrow slits in the sides and base of the bottle. Into each slit, push the knot of one of the arms and legs. It should stay inside on its own, but to make it more secure, you can dab the knot with a little bit of liquid glue before you push it in. Then hold the yarn slightly taut while the glue dries.

STEP 4

Cut out and glue colored card shapes to make your alien's head and face. You can make it as silly, slimy, scary, or strange as you like.

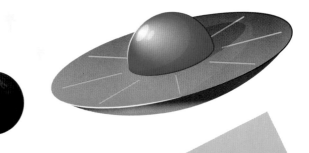

Cut two 20 inch lengths of thread and two 12 inch lengths of thread. Tie knots in the ends, and use a tiny dab of glue to stick one knot to the top of each of the alien's hands and feet, using the shorter threads for the hands and the longer threads for the feet.

STEP 6

Tie a short piece of thread around the middles of the straws to make an X shape. Tie the threads to the ends of the straws, so the legs are attached to one straw and the arms are attached to the other (use a dab of glue to make them extra secure). Stick on the head to complete your puppet.

BLEEP!

BLOOP!

19

GET-SET-GO JET PACK

Whether you're an astronaut on a mission to Mars or a superhero saving the city, this jet pack has got you covered. From blasting through space to zapping the evil aliens with the wrist gauntlets, is there anything this jet pack can't do?

YOU WILL NEED

- 2 two-liter bottles
- tissue paper
- liquid glue
- red and gold plastic film
- markers
- scissors
- sticky tape
- cardboard
- ribbon
- 2 16 oz bottles
- paint
- felt

STEP 1

Mix up one part liquid glue to one part water. Tear up strips of red and orange tissue paper and dip them into the glue mix. Paste them onto the two big bottles. Make sure you cover the bases of the bottles too.

STEP 2

Cut a long strip of the gold plastic film 2.5 inches thick. While the two bottles are still wet with glue, place them next to each other so that they stick together. Wrap the strip of plastic film around their middles (trim off any excess), then wait for the bottles to dry.

STEP 3

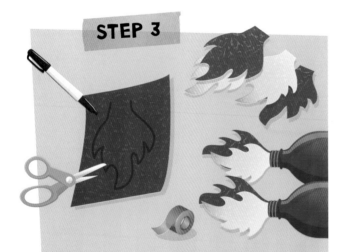

Draw flame shapes on the sheets of plastic film with a marker, then cut them out. Stick them inside the necks of the bottles using sticky tape.

STEP 4

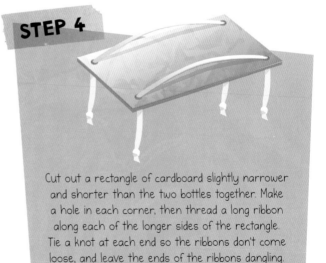

Cut out a rectangle of cardboard slightly narrower and shorter than the two bottles together. Make a hole in each corner, then thread a long ribbon along each of the longer sides of the rectangle. Tie a knot at each end so the ribbons don't come loose, and leave the ends of the ribbons dangling.

ZAAAP!

STEP 5

Spread liquid glue on the cardboard, and place the bottles onto it to stick them down. Wait for the glue to dry, then ask a grown-up to help you tie the ribbons comfortably, one over each shoulder, so you can wear the jet pack like a backpack.

STEP 7

STEP 6

To make the gauntlets, cut the tops and bottoms off the smaller bottles. Then cut a thin vertical strip away from the sides of the bottles, so that the bits that are left fit comfortably around your wrists.

Paint the gauntlets to decorate them. Then, when the paint is dry, draw on dials and buttons with colored markers. Cut a long strip of colored felt. Use it to cover the edges of the bottle, making sure no sharp bits are left. Stick the felt down with liquid glue.

OCTOPUS KITE

Turn the sky into an ocean of swimming sea creatures with these beautiful kites. Make sure you only fly them in a wide open space away from roads and powerlines.

YOU WILL NEED
- colorful plastic bag
- marker
- paint (optional)
- scissors
- 3 thin sticks
- sticky tape
- long string

STEP 1

Use a large plastic bag and draw the shape of your octopus head on it. Make it nice and big. Cut it out. If you want, you can use paint to draw a face.

STEP 2

Turn the octopus over and use sticky tape to attach the sticks to the back of the octopus' head.

STEP 3

Using the other side of the plastic bag, cut the handles off to make a rectangle. Trim the rectangle so it's the same width as the bottom of your octopus' head. Cut the bottom of the rectangle into eight dangling ribbons. Be careful not to cut all the way through the rectangle!

STEP 4

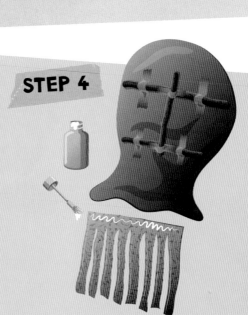

Spread liquid glue along the top of your strip of ribbons. Stick it to the bottom of the octopus' head and allow it to dry.

STEP 5

Tie the end of a ball of string to middle of the vertical stick. Attach the knot to the sticks with sticky tape to make it extra secure.

STEP 6 ⚠️

Take your kite to a safe, open outside area on a breezy day. Make sure you bring your grown-up with you. Then see how high your octopus can fly!

ECO THINGS

Don't throw old plastic away—transform it into something that gives the wildlife around you a helping hand instead. Invite birds to your garden or balcony with a tasty bird buffet, create a bug hotel that creepy-crawlies will love, or grow bee-friendly flowers in bee-utiful dangling plant hangers.

BUILD A BIRD FEEDER

Want more birds to visit your garden or balcony? Don't get in a flap. This super simple bird feeder will be the tweet of the town. Buy a bird seed mix from a garden center or pet shop, or mix up your own with sunflower seeds, uncooked oatmeal, dried fruit, and mild grated cheese.

YOU WILL NEED

- large juice carton
- marker
- scissors
- string
- short, thin twig
- liquid glue
- tissue paper
- bird seed

STEP 1

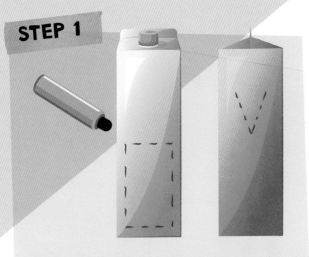

On the front of the juice carton, measure 0.5 inches in from the sides and 1 inch from the bottom, and draw a rectangle 4 inches tall. On each side of the juice carton, draw a V shape to be the bird's wings.

STEP 2

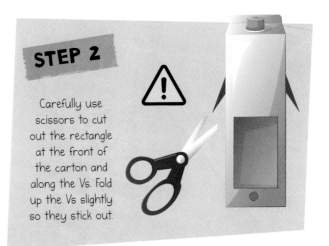

Carefully use scissors to cut out the rectangle at the front of the carton and along the Vs. Fold up the Vs slightly so they stick out.

STEP 3

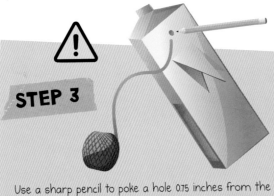

Use a sharp pencil to poke a hole 0.75 inches from the top of the carton in the middle of each side. Feed a length of string 12 inches long through the holes and tie it at the top. Then poke another hole in the front of the carton, under the cut-out rectangle.

STEP 4

Mix up one part of liquid glue to one part water. Dip the colored tissue paper into the mix and paste it over the carton, taking care not to cover the holes.

26

STEP 5

Paste glue over the top of the juice carton. Scrunch up pieces of tissue paper and stick them onto the carton.

It might take a little while for the birds to find the bird feeder. Keep it filled, and they'll find it soon!

TWEET!

STEP 6

Cut out shapes from a colorful plastic bag to make the eyes and beak and stick them on. Push the twig through the hole at the front of the birdfeeder to make a perch. Add seed and hang it up somewhere the birds can find it. Make sure it's more than 3 ft above the ground so cats can't catch the birds as they feed.

Check the food regularly to make sure it's still fresh and not moldy. Change the food often and wipe the inside of the bird feeder with a slightly soapy cloth to keep it clean.

In spring and summer, use tiny pinhead oats and soak any dried fruit overnight before you put it out, so that the food is small and soft enough for baby birds to eat safely.

BIRD-DAY BUFFET

Here are some more bird feeders to get your teeth (or should that be beak?) into. Different types of birdfeeder and bird food will attract different birds, so it's good to have a variety of options for your bird buffet.

STEP 1

Carefully cut a hole in the side of your plastic bottle, slightly larger than the handle of your plastic spoon, but smaller than the bowl of the spoon.

STEP 2

Slide a spoon through the hole. Where it hits the other side of the bottle, mark the point in marker and use scissors to cut a small hole. Push the end of the spoon through, so the bowl of the spoon is up against the bottle. Then repeat steps 1 and 2 with a second spoon.

For this type of feeder, you need a fine mix of bird seed. You can get this from a garden center or pet shop.

STEP 3

Carefully pour the birdseed up to the top of the bottle. As you pour, some birdseed should spill into the bowls of the spoons, making it easy for birds to reach. Replace the lid of the bottle and tie a loop of string around the lid, ready to hang it up.

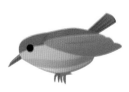

This high-fat, high-energy feeder is perfect winter fuel for birds. Make a big batch and keep them in the freezer. Hang up one or two at a time when the weather is cold, but don't use them in the spring or summer. If the fat melts, it can smear on the birds' wings and make it tricky for them to fly.

STEP 1

Use a sharp pencil or ask a grown-up to use a knife to make a small hole in the bottom of the yogurt cup.

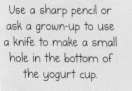

STEP 2

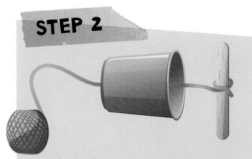

Thread the string through the hole. Tie the end of the string to the plastic spoon or twig. This will be the perch for the birds to stand on while they eat.

STEP 3

Pour the cubes of fat into the mixing bowl. Add the other ingredients—you should have about twice as much of the other ingredients as you have of the fat.

STEP 4

Use your hands to squish the fat and the other ingredients together. The warmth from your hands should melt the fat slightly, making it easier to mix.

STEP 5

Fill the yogurt cups with the mix, then leave them in the fridge overnight. Slide off or cut away the yogurt cups from the fat cake, then use the string to hang up the cakes somewhere the birds can find them.

✻ Currants and sultanas are toxic to dogs, so don't use them in gardens where dogs come to visit.

CRUNCHY CRESSHEADS

Give these cressheads a silly hairstyle. Decorate them however you like—you could even make a set of them that looks like you and your family. When the cress is grown, you can snip it off and eat it in a sandwich or salad. Crunch!

Keep your cressheads on a sunny windowsill to help the cress grow.

STEP 1

Make sure your yogurt cup is clean and dry. Paint the outside of your yogurt cup. Use brown or orange to make a puppy.

STEP 2

While the paint on the yogurt cup dries, cut ears, eyes, a nose, a mouth, and a tongue from scraps of fabric or an old T-shirt (check with your grown-up first!).

STEP 3

Use liquid glue to stick the fabric shapes onto the yogurt cup to make your puppy's face. Stick the ears just inside the yogurt cup so they flop out over the edge.

While your cress is growing, keep checking the cotton balls. If they dry out, sprinkle more water over them.

Your cress should be ready to harvest after about 2-3 weeks.

YOU WILL NEED

- yogurt cup
- paint
- colored fabric scraps
- liquid glue
- cotton balls
- cotton pad
- cress seeds

Cut up a colored sponge to make fluffy clown hair.

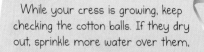

STEP 4

Fill the inside of the yogurt cup with cotton balls, then add a flat cotton pad or folded square of paper towel on top. You may need to cut it so it fits neatly.

STEP 5

Scatter the cress seeds on top of the cotton pad. Lightly sprinkle a little bit of water over the top, just enough to soak through all the cotton without it sloshing at the bottom. Then wait for your cress to grow.

31

BIG FLOWER BUG HOTEL

Beetles, bugs, and creepy-crawlies all help to keep the environment healthy, and they all need little nooks and crannies to hide in. Pack this flower-shaped bug hotel with lots of things from the garden or park to make it a 5-star luxury place to stay for all sorts of bugs.

YOU WILL NEED

- 7 two-liter bottles
- tissue paper
- liquid glue
- stapler
- hole punch
- string
- a mix of:
  - little pine cones
  - short twigs
  - rolled-up cardboard
  - newspaper
  - dry leaves
  - gravel

STEP 1

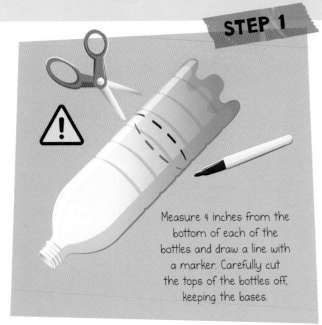

Measure 4 inches from the bottom of each of the bottles and draw a line with a marker. Carefully cut the tops of the bottles off, keeping the bases.

STEP 2

Mix up one part liquid glue to one part water. Dip colored strips of tissue paper in the glue mix and paste them onto the bottle bottoms to decorate them.

STEP 3

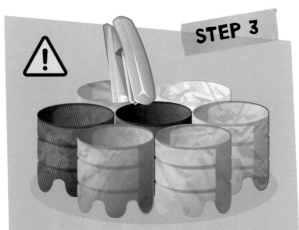

When the glue is dry, arrange the bottle bottoms into a flower shape. Use a stapler to join the bottles together wherever they touch.

STEP 4

Use a hole punch to make two holes in the sides of each of the outer bottle bottoms.

STEP 5

Thread the string in and out of the holes, so the string wraps around the outside of the flower. Tie the two ends together, leaving plenty of loose string to let you hang up the finished bug hotel.

STEP 6

Place a pencil across the corner of a sheet of newspaper and roll it up tightly. Carefully pull the pencil out without unrolling the newspaper, trim the tubes to 4 inches long, and pack them lengthwise into one of the flower sections.

STEP 7

Gather the rest of your garden things and fill up each of the sections of your flower. Use a different thing in each section to encourage lots of different bugs to visit.

WINDOWSILL WATER GARDEN

STEP 1

Measure 6 inches from the top of a plastic bottle and draw a line around the bottle. Use scissors to cut the top of the bottle off.

Grow flowers and crops whatever the weather with this windowsill water garden, perfect for packing a lot of plants into a small space. Grow beautiful flowers, or keep herbs like chives, parsley, or basil in your kitchen so they're easy to use on pizzas and pasta.

STEP 2

Mix one part liquid glue to one part water. Dip pieces of tissue paper into the glue mix and paste them onto the bottom part of the bottle. Cut some colourful shapes out of tissue paper and arrange them on the bottle to make flowers, butterflies, and bugs.

STEP 3

Ask an adult to punch a hole in the lid of the bottle about 0.5 inches wide. Measure 12 inches of string, but don't cut it. Instead, loop it around, so you have several lengths of 12 inches, until the bundle is 0.5 inches thick. Then cut the string. Feed it through the hole in the lid, and pull it so it's halfway through.

STEP 4

Pull the loops of string inside the top part of the bottle apart from each other. Pour the coir or sphagnum moss around them, so the strings are evenly spread inside the bottle top.

Quick-growing plant seeds work best for this, like lettuce, chives, daisies, and marigolds.

YOU WILL NEED

- two-liter plastic bottle
- marker
- scissors
- tissue paper
- liquid glue
- string
- coir or sphagnum moss✱
- liquid plant food
- flower seeds

✱ You can get these from a garden center.

STEP 5

When the glue has dried, pour water into the bottom part of the bottle so it's about half full. Add a couple of drops of plant food and swish lightly to mix.

STEP 6

Carefully place the top of the bottle inside the bottom of the bottle. It should rest inside with the string dangling into the water. Plant some seeds according to the instructions on the pack, and place the planter somewhere sunny and cool.

HANGING PLANTERS

Fill these colorful dangling planters with bees' and butterflies' favorite flowers to encourage them to visit. The pollen and nectar will give the bugs a tasty snack. Nasturtiums, marigolds, and crocuses are all perfect for pollinators.

STEP 1

Measure 6 inches from the top of a bottle. Draw a line with a marker around the bottle, then cut the top off the bottle. Take off the lid and ask a grown-up to use a hammer and nail to poke a large hole in it.

STEP 2

Turn the bottle upside down, so the lid is at the bottom and the cut edge is at the top. Use a hole punch to make three holes around the top.

STEP 3

Tie a length of string into each hole. Check your seed packet to find out the maximum height of your plant, and make sure you make the strings longer than that. Leave one of the strings longer than the other two. Tie the strings at the top, using the longer string to make a loop to hang your planter.

36

Some succulents, like sedum, are great for butterflies. Their fat, chunky leaves store a supply of water, so they're perfect for places the rain doesn't reach.

YOU WILL NEED

- two-liter plastic bottle
- scissors
- holepunch
- string
- tissue paper
- liquid glue
- colored card
- potting compost
- plant seeds

STEP 5

While the glue on your planter is still sticky, cut out shapes from coloured card to decorate the planter. You can make a flower pattern, polka dots or whatever you want. Paint a layer of liquid glue over the top—this makes a waterproof seal against the rain.

STEP 4

Make up a mix of one part liquid glue to one part water. Tear up strips of tissue paper and dip them in the mix, then paste them onto the planter.

STEP 6

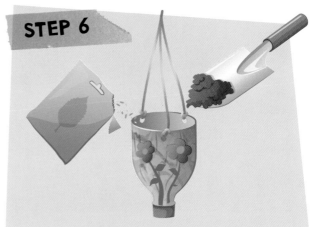

Fill your planter with garden soil or compost. Plant the seeds according to the directions on the packet. Choose plants that are happy in hanging baskets, and ones that bees and butterflies love.

DECORATIONS

Whether it's a party day or
just every day, these plastic crafts
are perfect for brightening things up. From a
flowery summer wreath to apple snack boxes,
you can turn old plastic into something
that looks fantastic.

SUPER STREAMERS

Every party is better with streamers. Make these beautiful decorations out of reused plastic bags. The brighter and more colorful the bags, the better!

YOU WILL NEED

- brightly colored plastic bags
- card
- marker
- scissors
- liquid glue
- long ribbon or string

STEP 1

Draw a triangular stencil on card and cut it out. Place it with the short side against the folded edge of the bag and draw around it with a marker. Arrange as many as possible on the bag, then cut them out.

STEP 2

Unfold a triangle to make a kite shape. Paste glue onto one half of the kite. Make sure you get glue right up to the fold line.

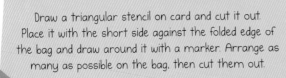

STEP 3

Tie a loop on the end of the ribbon. Carefully place the ribbon on the fold line of the kite shape. Fold the kite in half to make a triangle shape again, sandwiching the ribbon so it sticks to the glue. Leave a short gap, then attach the next triangle to the ribbon in the same way, mixing up the colors as you go.

STEP 4

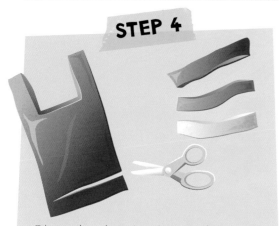

Take another plastic bag. Cut it into horizontal strips 1 inch wide. Cut along one side of each strip and unfold it so it's twice the length. Do this with three different colored plastic bags.

STEP 5

Take a strip in each color, and bundle them together so the ends line up. Fold them loosely in half, and wrap the folded ends around the ribbon to make a loop. Feed the dangling ends through the loop and pull tight. Alternate triangles and ribbons until your streamers are the length you want, then cut the ribbon and tie another loop in it so you can hang it up.

SUMMER WREATH

Whether you're having a sunny garden party or brightening up your room in the middle of winter, this flower wreath will make it feel like summer every day.

YOU WILL NEED

- 4 mini yogurt bottles
- scrap colour fabric
- marker
- scissors
- green card
- cardboard
- liquid glue

STEP 1

Draw around the bottom of a bottle onto the scrap fabric. Cut out the circle. Repeat 3 more times, so you have a circle for each of the bottles. Then flip the bottle over and draw around the lid instead. Cut out four lid-sized circles of fabric, so you have eight circles in total.

STEP 2

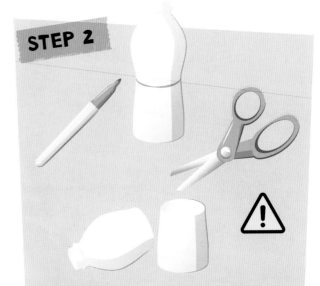

Draw a line around the middle of one of the bottles, then cut it in half. Do this with all of the bottles.

STEP 3

Use the marker to draw lines down the sides of the bottle halves. Try to make sure that all the lines are a similar distance apart. Use scissors to cut along the lines, then cut around each of the strips to round them off into petal shapes.

STEP 4

Draw leaf shapes onto stiff green scrap fabric or card, then cut them out. 24 leaves will give you three leaves per flower.

STEP 5

Draw around a large dinner plate onto the cardboard. Place a smaller plate inside the circle, then draw around it to make a ring shape. Cut out the ring. Make a hole 0.75 inches from its edge, using a sharp pencil to punch through the cardboard (do this onto something like sticky tack or plasticine to make it easier).

STEP 6

For each flower, arrange three leaves on the ring and stick them down with liquid glue. Paint glue onto the bottom or lid of a bottle and stick that on top of the leaves. Finally, dab some glue inside the bottle, and put the fabric circle inside to make the middle of the flower. Make sure you don't cover the hole in the ring.

STEP 7

When the glue is dry, tie a ribbon through the hole you made, and hang up your wreath wherever you like.

You can make this wreath as big as you like. Just use more yogurt bottles and a bigger circle of cardboard.

For an extra colorful variation, paint the plastic bottles before you cut the petal shapes.

APPLE SNACK BOXES

How do you make an apple turnover? Roll it down a hill!
How do you make an apple snack box? Just follow these
instructions. These mini apple boxes are perfect for
keeping dried fruits and nuts for lunchtime snacks,
or for using as little gift boxes.

YOU WILL NEED

- 2 two-liter bottles
- marker
- scissors
- paint
- holepunch and ribbon
  OR
- a zipper just shorter
  than the bottle's
  circumference
- green scrap fabric
- twig
- liquid glue

STEP 1

You'll need two plastic bottles for each box. Measure
2 inches from the bottom of the bottles and draw lines
around them. On one bottle, cut along the line so you
have a flat edge. On the other bottle, against the line
you've just drawn, draw a square 1 inch x 1 inch. Cut
along the line, going around the square to make a tab.

STEP 2

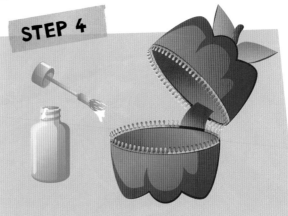

Paint the bottle bottoms. If you're not going to use
your boxes to hold food, you can paint the inside of
the bottle so the outside stays shiny.

STEP 3

If you don't have a
zipper, skip these steps
and go onto step 5!

Once the paint is dry, paint a line of glue around the
inside edges of both bottle bottoms. Stick one side of
the zipper to the inside of one of the bottle bottoms,
so the end of the zipper is next to the plastic tab. Take
care to keep the line of the zipper straight.

STEP 4

Dab some glue on the outer side of the tab.
Unzip the zipper. Turn the other bottle bottom
upside down and stick it carefully to the tab
and to the other side of the zipper.

STEP 5

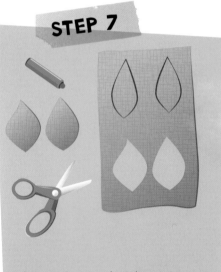

If you don't have a zipper, use a hole punch to make two holes 1 inch apart on each of the bottle bottoms. On the bottle bottom with the tab, make sure the holes are on the opposite side to the tab.

STEP 6

Dab some glue on the outer side of the tab, then turn the other bottle bottom upside down and stick the tab to its inside. Make sure the holes at the front line up.

STEP 7

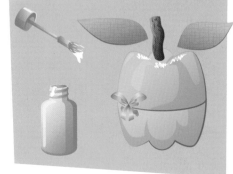

Draw and cut out leaf shapes from the scrap fabric. Find a short twig, and use liquid glue to stick it and the leaves to the top of the apple. If not using a zipper, cut a 8-inch ribbon and thread it through the holes on both apples, tying it in a bow to finish.

YUM!

SECRET MONEY BOX

These clever crafts look like silly creatures, but peek behind their hungry mouths and you'll find a secret slot to hide away your money. Perfect for saving for a rainy day.

CHA-CHING!

STEP 1

Use the marker to draw a slot 1.5 inches long and 0.5 inches wide across the front of your plastic bottle. Use scissors to carefully cut it out.

STEP 2

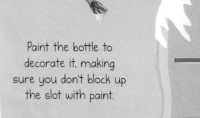

Paint the bottle to decorate it, making sure you don't block up the slot with paint.

STEP 3

Draw wing shapes onto some colored plastic film, the sort you get when you buy flowers. Cut them out and stick them onto the back of the bottle.

STEP 4

When the paint on the bottle is dry, cut a piece of sticky tape to the same length as the slot. Slide it half into the slot, fold it over the bottom edge and stick it down. Do this again with the top edge of the slot. This keeps the edges from being sharp.

Draw shapes on colored card and scrap fabric to decorate your money box and stick them on with liquid glue. Use fabric to make the mouth. Put a line of glue over the top of the slot, and stick the fabric to it, so it hides the slot but so that you can lift the mouth up to slide your money through the slot.

GULP!

Use unusually shaped bottles and different color paints to make different animals.

Blue paint and a giant mouth makes this hippo look super hungry!

Use green paint and make pointy ears out of stiff fabric to make a hungry alien.

OM NOM NOM!

STAINED GLASS SUNCATCHERS

Hang these beautiful stained glass suncatchers by a sunny window. When the sun shines through them, your room will be filled with beams of rainbow light.

YOU WILL NEED

- stiff black card
- white pencil or chalk
- scissors
- clear plastic bag or plastic film
- liquid glue
- see-through colored plastic candy wrappers
- colored ribbon or sticky tack

STEP 1

Draw your bug shapes onto black card with a white pencil. Make them quite big, at least 6 inches across, so you have plenty of space for the stained glass effect.

STEP 2

Around the edges of the bugs' wings, or any other areas you want to use for the stained glass, measure 0.75 inches in and draw a line, following the outside line, so you have a 0.75 inch border all the way around.

STEP 3

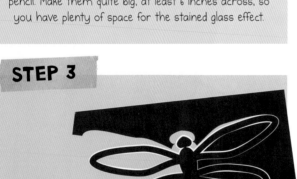

Carefully cut out your bug shapes. Cut out the wings from inside the bugs, leaving the 0.75 inch border and the bugs' bodies intact.

STEP 4

Lay your plastic cellophane flat. Paste liquid glue onto the bug shape, making sure you cover all of the border. Stick the bug shape onto the cellophane, making sure you don't get any wrinkles in the plastic.

OOOH!

STEP 5

STEP 6

Gather your candy wrappers and use the liquid glue to stick them over the bug's wings. Try overlapping them to get different colors and effects. Keep going until the bug's wings are covered, with no gaps.

When the glue is dry, use scissors to cut around the bug shape, cutting off the extra plastic film and bits of candy wrapper. Use sticky tack to stick the bug to a window, or use liquid glue to attach a colored ribbon so you can hang it somewhere sunny.

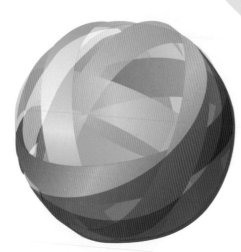

QUICK CRAFTS

Here are some super simple crafts
with super impressive results!

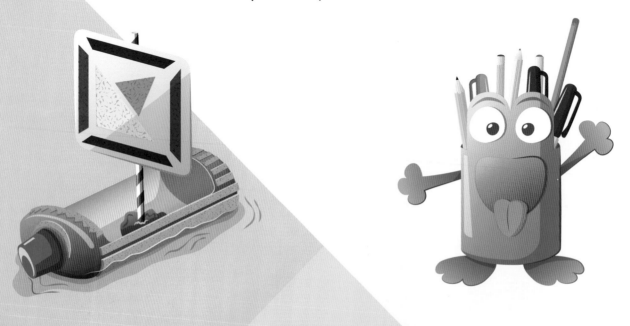

TWIRLERS

These rainbow wind catchers make a lovely garden decoration. Hang them somewhere the breeze will make them whirl and twirl.

STEP 1

Before you start, unscrew the bottle lids and ask a grown-up to use a nail and hammer to punch a hole in each lid. Screw the lids back on. Then use the markers to draw colorful patterns on the plastic bottles.

STEP 2

Use scissors to cut off the bottom of the bottle, then cut around the sides in a spiral shape.

STEP 3

Fold a 20-inch length of string in half. Thread the two ends through the hole in one of the bottle lids. Then thread them through the second bottle lid, sliding the top of the bottle up inside the first bottle. Repeat with the third bottle, then tie a knot in the ends of the string. Use the loop to hang the twirler somewhere breezy.

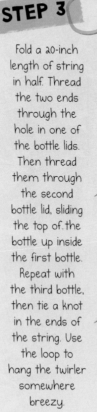

YOU WILL NEED

- 3 identical plastic bottles
- colored permanent markers
- scissors
- string

MONSTER PEN POTS

These monsters hate messy desks! They'll munch up all your pens and pencils and keep them neat and tidy.

YOU WILL NEED
- plastic bottles
- marker
- scissors
- paint
- liquid glue
- colored card

STEP 1

Make sure your bottle is almost as tall as your pens and pencils so it can hold them without toppling over. Draw around the top of the bottle. Use spiky lines for a scary monster or blobby lines for a silly monster.

STEP 2

Carefully cut along the top of the bottle where you drew the line. Then paint your monsters and wait for them to dry.

STEP 3

Cut out cardboard shapes to turn your pen pots into monsters. Don't forget to give them tentacles or arms, and you can even cut out feet shapes and stick them to the bottom of the pen pot.

ANIMAL PLANTERS

You can also use old bottles to make mini plant pots to decorate your room. Try these ones below.

YOU WILL NEED

- plastic bottles
- marker
- scissors
- paint
- liquid glue
- colored card
- tin foil
- scrap fabric
- compost
- small houseplant or seeds

STEP 1

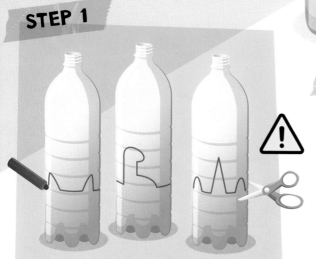

Draw your animal shape on the bottle—include a spiky horn and ears for a unicorn, pointy ears for an owl, or a long neck for a dinosaur. Cut out the shapes, then ask a grown-up to poke several holes in the bottom of the bottle.

STEP 2

Decorate the plant pots with paint and colored card. You can use tin foil to make a shiny horn for the unicorn. Make feathers for the owl by cutting scrap fabric into mini semicircles, then stick them to the bottle with liquid glue in overlapping rows.

STEP 3

When the paint and glue are dry, pour some compost into your planters. Repot a small houseplant from a garden center, or grow your own from seeds, following the instructions on the seed packet.

53

QUICK FOOTBALL

This plastic football is a great way to reuse old plastic bags, plus it never goes flat!

YOU WILL NEED

- lots of plastic bags
- string
- scissors

STEP 1

Stuff several plastic bags inside another plastic bag. Bundle them up tightly—when they're scrunched up, they should be a bit smaller than a football.

STEP 2

Wind string around the outside of the scrunched-up bundle of bags. Make it as round as possible, but don't worry about any lumps and bumps.

STEP 3

Make a long ribbon by cutting around another plastic bag. You'll need more than one plastic bag for this, so each time you run out, cut another one the same way.

STEP 4

Wrap the ribbon around the ball, making sure the ribbon lies flat against the ball's surface. Keep wrapping until the ball is round and smooth. When you reach the end of one ribbon, tuck the end tightly underneath the next ribbon. When you're ready to finish, tie the last bit of ribbon to another, more secure ribbon or use liquid glue to stick it to the ball's surface.

BOTTLE BOATS

These boats actually float. Make more than one and race them along a stream, or see which one can carry the heaviest cargo.

STEP 1

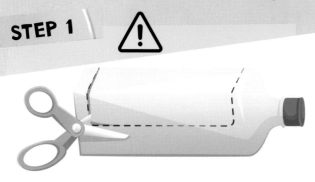

Lay the bottle on its side. Measure halfway up the sides of the bottle and 0.75 inches from the top and bottom of the bottle. Draw a rectangle over the sides and front of the bottle. Cut it out and discard.

STEP 2

Decorate the side of the boat with the candy wrappers, sticking them down with liquid glue in whatever pattern you like.

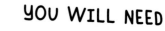

STEP 3

Draw a rectangle on the larger side of the milk bottle and cut it out. Decorate one side of it with more candy wrappers to make your boat's sail. Wait for the glue to dry.

STEP 4

Attach the straw to the back of your sail with sticky tape. Put a lump of sticky tack inside of the boat, then push the straw into the sticky tack, squishing the sticky tack up the sides of the straw to make it secure.

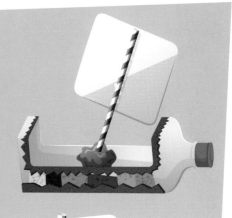

Make sure you only sail your boat in safe places with your grown-up nearby!

BIG CRAFTS

These crafts might take a
bit longer to finish, but the
results will be worth it . . .

SECRET GARDEN HIDEAWAY

Sssh! This secret hideaway is just for kids. It's the perfect den for secret meetings or for using as a reading nook on long summer days. Make sure you choose somewhere safe and flat before you start building.

YOU WILL NEED

- 6 long garden canes
- colorful plastic bags (you'll need a lot!)
- 15 large pebbles
- 1 short stick or twig
- sticky tape
- string

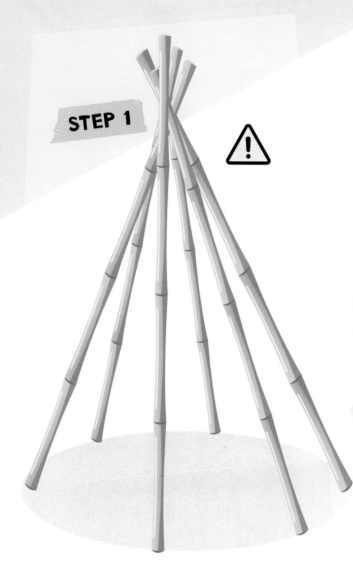

STEP 1

Set up the garden canes in a cone shape, so the canes are evenly spaced. Ask an adult to help you. When they're in position, get your grown-up to push them into the ground so they're secure.

STEP 2

Use string to tightly tie the tops of the garden canes together, so they're secure. Get your grown-up to check that the structure of the hideaway is safe and secure.

STEP 3

Prepare the ribbons made out of the plastic bags. You'll need lots of these. Cut along the bottom of a plastic bag and keep going around the bottom to turn each bag into one long ribbon about 1.5 inches wide.

STEP 4

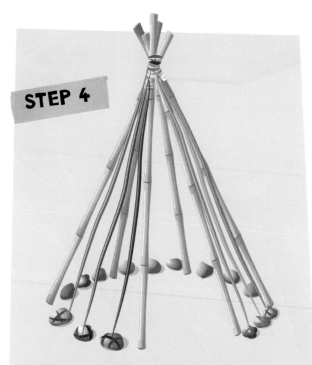

Take a long plastic ribbon and tie one end around the top of the hideaway. Let the other end fall to the ground. Tie it to a rock so it stays taut and in position. Repeat this all the way around the hideaway so there are 3 ribbons and rocks in each gap between the canes. Leave a gap at the front for the entrance.

STEP 5

Starting at the top of the hideaway, tie the end of a ribbon to one of the canes by the entrance. Weave the ribbon under and over the other ribbons and canes all the way around the hideaway.

STEP 7

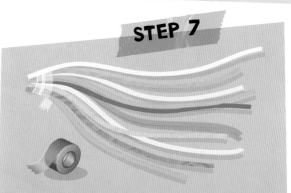

Gather any leftover bits of ribbon and trim them to the same length. Wind sticky tape around the bundle tightly to keep them together.

Divide the bundle of ribbons into two and thread a piece of string between the two bundles. Use another piece of sticky tape to secure the string against the sticky tape already around the ribbons. Tie the string to the top of the twig. Feed the twig into the top of the hideaway, tying it securely in place.

STEP 6

When you get to the end of one ribbon, tie the end to the nearest cane, and keep going with another ribbon. Keep going around the hideaway until you reach the bottom.

58

Use different colored plastic bags to make different themed hideaways. Collect black and gold bags and make a skull-and-crossbones flag for a pirate hideaway, or pretty pastel colors for a fairy hideaway.

Tie extra bundles of ribbons to the sides to decorate your hideaway.

WEARABLE PIRATE SHIP

Ahoy there and shiver me timbers! Be the captain of your very own pirate ship, big enough to sit inside or wear over your shoulders.

PIECES OF EIGHT!

YE BE NEEDIN'

- large cardboard box
- marker
- scissors
- six blue plastic lids
- brown plastic food trays
- liquid glue
- blue plastic bag
- packing tape
- large white milk bottle
- black card
- newspaper
- thin garden cane
- white trash bag
- stapler

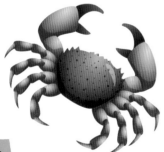

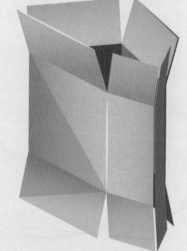

Unfold the top and bottom of the box and check it's big enough to easily slip over your head and shoulders. Cut straight down the middle of the front of the box. Bend the two sides inward so the cut edges make a point at the front. Secure them temporarily with masking tape.

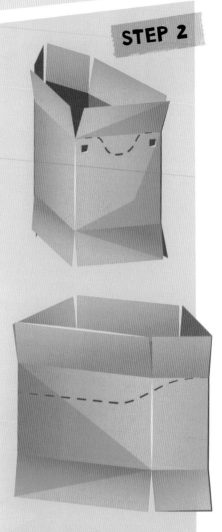

Draw along the back and sides of the box to make a pirate ship shape. The front of the ship should bend upward on each side to make the bow. Cut along the lines you've just drawn and trim the flaps off the bottom of the ship. Keep the cardboard flaps you've just cut off for later. Make two small holes in the back of the ship.

STEP 3

Remove the masking tape and flatten the ship to make it easier to work on. Use your blue lids to make portholes (if you can't find blue lids, use whatever color you have and paint them). Stick three to each side of the ship.

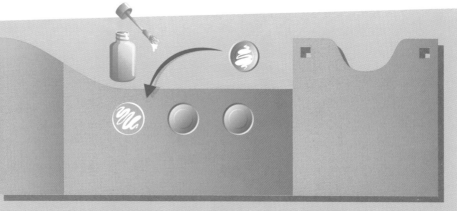

STEP 4

Cut up your brown plastic food trays into lots of rectangles of different sizes.

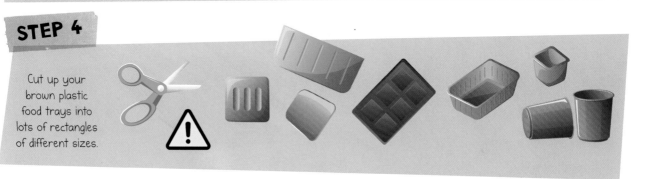

SQUAWK!

STEP 5

Use liquid glue to stick the brown plastic rectangles to one side of your ship. Arrange them neatly so they look like the wooden boards of a ship, making sure you don't cover the holes from step 2.

STEP 6

Take your blue plastic bag and cut a long strip from it 6 inches wide. Cut lines ¾ of the way across the width to make a fringe.

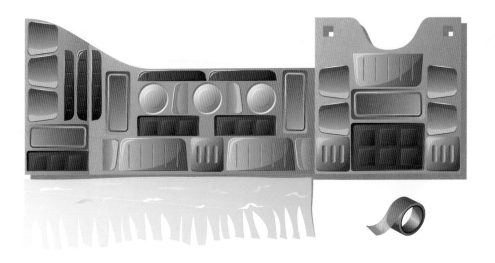

Use packing tape to attach the fringe at the bottom of the ship to make the rippling waves. Wait for the glue to dry, then repeat steps 5-7 on the other side of your ship.

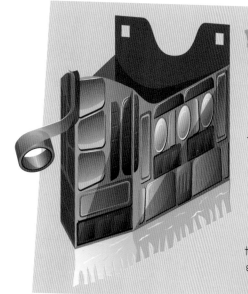

STEP 8

Stand your ship upright and bring the two cut edges together to make a point again. This time, use a long strip of packing tape to join the two sides together.

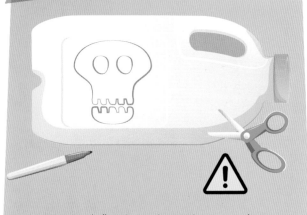

STEP 9

Draw a skull and crossbones design on a large, white milk bottle. Carefully cut it out.

STEP 10

Paste your skull and crossbones design onto a sheet of black card to make your flag.

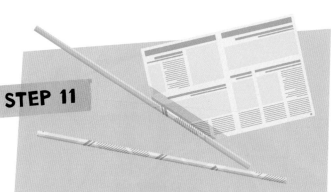

STEP 11

Take a large sheet of newspaper and a narrow garden cane. Place the cane diagonally across the corner of the newspaper sheet and tightly wrap the cane in the newspaper. Secure it with sticky tape, then slide the cane out of the newspaper roll. Make three of these rolls.

STEP 12

Attach one newspaper roll to your pirate flag with sticky tape. Then slide it inside the front of the pirate ship and secure it with some more sticky tape.

STEP 13

Cut a T shape out of cardboard to make your mast. Stick the wide part inside the back of your ship. At the top and bottom of the mast, stick the other newspaper rolls so they make two crossbars.

STEP 14

Take your large, white plastic trash bag and cut along the side and bottom. Unfold it to make a large white rectangle. Trim the edges to make it just narrower than your newspaper crossbars and shorter than your mast.

STEP 15

Fold the top of the sail over the newspaper crossbar and staple the two layers of plastic together. Do the same at the bottom of the sail.

STEP 16

On the bow of the ship, where the fold lines of the box are, measure the width of the ship. Cut a rectangle of cardboard slightly longer than the width of the ship. If you want to wear your ship, make two holes in the rectangle. Fold the sides down at a slight diagonal, so the cardboard slots neatly into the front of the ship, then stick it in place to reinforce the front of the ship. Wait for the glue to dry.

If you want to wear your ship, ask your grown-up to tie two long pieces of ribbon through the holes in the back and front of the ship, so there's one long ribbon either side. Your grown-up should check that the ship will be safe and comfortable to wear. Then slide the ship over your head, so you have one ribbon over each shoulder like a vest top, and set sail for adventure!

AHOY MATEY!

ARRR!